The Girl from Greece

An Italian Soldier's Story of Surviving World War II

Alessandro Rasile
and
Dustin Lawson

The Girl from Greece

An Italian Soldier's Story of Surviving World War II

This book is dedicated to my wife, Rosa Rasile. After I went through so much suffering during and after the war she gave me joy. She gave me life. We were married for almost 68 years. She died on May 2, 2017.

This book is also for my dear friend, Tommasso Palma. We met as prisoners. The bond of our friendship could never be broken. This book is also for my family, the greatest reward of my life. When I look at a family picture I cannot help but think about all the generations that would have never existed if I had not survived the war.

I would like to thank my son, John Rasile, for his work translating my journal and performing background research. His efforts greatly aided in the completion of this project.

Lastly, this book is for all my brothers who fought with me in the 33rd Division, Acqui. This story is as much theirs as it is mine. May this book stand as a testament to their sacrifice.

ALESSANDRO RASILE

Foreword

By Captain John Mingo

I will never forget the first time my grandfather told me about the war. I was no more than six years old. He sat down with my brother and I at our home. While we were playing, he said, "Your mother wants me to tell you about my time in the war."

As we sat, surrounded by plastic army men, grandpa briefly shared with us that he had fought in a war when he was young. He did not share everything with us because, as he said, "You are too young."

I knew from this brief exchange that my grandfather had done something extraordinary, and I wanted to be like him. From that point on I knew that one day I would also be a soldier. I also hoped to learn the details of my grandfather's story.

As I grew older and joined the military, my grandfather did share with me more of his wartime experience. But, he did not tell me everything that is in this book.

I hope that anyone who takes the time to learn his story will hold an appreciation for the soldiers of the 33rd Acqui division. They were men who followed orders. But, when given the chance to decide what side of a World War they were on, they opted to fight for liberty instead of tyranny.

TABLE of CONTENTS

ALESSANDRO RASILE

Alessandro drew this map of the Greek island of Cephalonia.

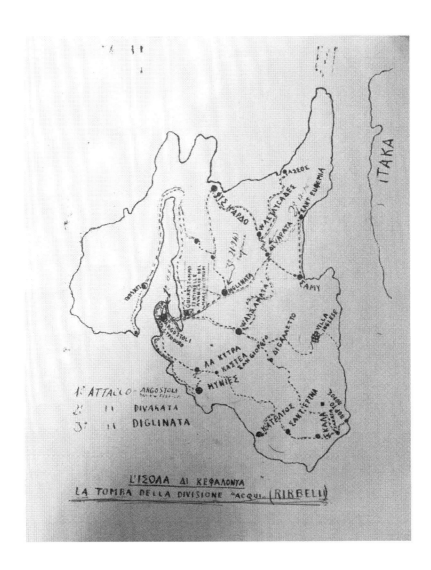

INTRODUCTION
The Accident

Manhattan, 1968

One day, twenty-three years after the war, Alessandro was on his way home from Lourdes Dress Company where he worked as a presser. Lourdes was located at 34th Street and 9th Avenue.

He crossed a street.

The light turned green.

A car in the third lane farthest from Alessandro did not realize people were still crossing the street. It sped forward, hitting Alessandro and throwing him across the road into oncoming traffic. He was taken to Saint Clair's Hospital. His leg was broken. The cast covered his entire leg.

While his leg was being put into traction, a nurse intern walked into Alessandro's room. When she saw him, she looked surprised. She smiled and said, "I recognize you."

Alessandro had no idea who she was.

ALESSANDRO RASILE

ONE

Taking My Friends Place

At the age of seventeen, I took a course under the official military school in Casagiove Province of Caserta, Naples. After successfully passing the exam, I was promoted to sergeant. Later, I was promoted to staff sergeant. I was then assigned to the 34th Infantry Regiment in Fosano Province of Cunero.

Then, as fate or chance would have it, the Second World War began.

So began my story of tragedy and triumph.

We were stationed on Mont Blanc. This was the highest mountain in the Alpine Range. It would snow all day, even in June.

We were on guard to keep the French from crossing the Alps and invading Italy. Thankfully, the days in the mountains were few. Eventually, we returned to the barracks in Fosano.

I was later sent to Alexandria to instruct soldiers on how to use the new weapons.

After three months in Alexandria as an instructor, I returned to Caserta barracks in Fosano. Later, I was assigned to command a team of Explorers. My job was to teach them how to read topographic maps and work communication devices.

While at Caserta, I became friends with a sergeant named Aldo Sturaro. A cheerful guy, Sergeant Sturaro played three instruments: the violin, mandolin and guitar. In the evenings after work, we would meet with friends in taverns or restuarants to drink Chianti, a specialty of Piedmont.

Later that year, in October 1940, the war between Greece and Italy began. During this time, the 17th Infantry Division fought. This division suffered huge losses. The losses were so great that reinforcements had to be taken from other regiments in Italy.

I received orders to train my regiment for war. My friend, Sturaro, was included in the group. The next day, I gave my friend the news that we were heading to war.

Sturaro was upset because he was married and had a five-year-old girl.

I said, "Do not worry because I am going to volunteer in your place."

He hugged me and said, "Thank you. I won't forget you."

TWO

Attacking the Greeks

The next day, I was given command of the group. I was responsible to accompany them to the Regiment in Albania. We left the same day I was put in command.

It was night when we arrived in Valona, Albania. From the landing place, we had to walk three kilometers to reach the city. While in the city we found the regimental headquarters. I turned over the one hundred soldiers who were to be assigned to the 17th infantry.

In the Regimental Command Office, the Colonel ordered that the 100 new soldiers be given whatever provisions they needed. That next morning, we were accompanied by a mountain regiment.

After being in the mountains for three months, on Holy Saturday, we received orders to attack the Greeks. The following day, the Greeks retreated towards Porta Edda. There, they took to the sea and landed at Corfu.

We followed them.

When we arrived, the Greeks had fled to the mountains. For three months, we managed to re-establish order in Corfu.

After those three months, we were sent to Cephalonia with the same task of establishing order.

We spent twenty-nine months in peace on the island of Cephalonia. We were there until the fall of Mussolini on July 23, 1943.

THREE

Allies Become Enemies

On the evening of the 8th of September 1943, the armistice of Italy was announced. Marshall Badoglio issued the following press release:

"The Italian soldiers, wherever they are held tight in its' (Germany's) fist, will use their weapons and will attack anyone who should attack us."

The following day, we had orders to keep ready and be alert against the Germans. There were about two thousand German soldiers on the island with us.

Our camp was located close to an olive grove near the Castel S. Giorgio, four kilometers from the town of ARGOSTOLI.

In the afternoon of the 10th, the Commander of the Battalion Altavilla Oscarradioed said, "The Germans have proposed that we lay down our arms and want us to concentrate our troops at one point on the island. Within hours, they will expedite us by neutral steamers back to Italy.

"I did not believe that any soldier of my Battalion would be fooled by this proposal and let their weapon fall into the deception of the Germans. However, those who accept their proposal come out from the ranks."

No one moved. All murmured, "Hurry, there's no time to lose."

Within minutes, we loaded the ammunition on the trucks. While waiting for orders, we started to take positions on the peripherals of the city. On the evening of the 14th, the Commander of the Brigade issued the order to reform within our respective divisions.

My company, commanded by Captain Ciaiolo, executed the order. While marching to that location, we encountered a roadblock that had been set up by drunken sailors to confiscate weapons. The company, including the captain, was stopped and held at gunpoint. A group of soldiers and I escaped.

I went to the Regimental Commander and reported the incident to the Colonel who, without wasting time, put at my disposal a vehicle with a rifle team. I then left to free my company. But, upon arrival, I discovered that the company had already been freed.

On the morning of the 15th came the order to load ammunitions and personnel on the trucks. In less than two hours, the whole Battalion was deployed and ready to attack the German command located in St. Theodore.

We waited in anticipation for the order to attack.

In the afternoon came a German maritime aircraft. It was at low altitude and heading towards the mouth of the Bay of LIXURI. Italian troops, without receiving the order, opened fire.

Despite the fire, the plane was still able to land.

After a few minutes, two troop-landing crafts came to the mouth of the port. Our batteries waited for the ships to come into port. But, before the first could dock, our batteries opened fire. After a few blasts, the boat was shattered.

The second troop-landing craft was still at the mouth of the port. After being hit at various points, it decided to raise the white flag.

My team and I had already been given standing orders, assigned automatic weapons, and given designated shooting sectors. We had orders to hold position as lookouts. Unless there was an order to attack, the others had to stay fifty meters behind the line. I ran from one location to another checking the weapons.

The area where we were deployed was a strip of land, 600 meters by 1000 meters. On it was a scattering of weapons of all calibers.

Eventually, taking us by surprise, there was a clattering of engines flying over us.

It was forty stukas!

The Germans began to rain down bombs, followed by continued bursts of machine guns. I managed to throw myself to the ground between two rocks. I was unable to raise my head because of everything raining down. The batteries fired furiously. There were cries of wounded soldiers. It was hell.

I was almost buried by the soil thrown up by the bombs. I decided to go for it, and took off running for the command post of the company to receive orders.

In a moment of calm, I raised my head.

I couldn't see anyone. Despite the incessant rain of bombs, everyone escaped. Some had taken refuge among the rocks by the sea.

The Commander of the Battalion was hit by a bomb. Dead bodies were scattered among the shattered tents.

I didn't know where to go or what to do. The German ground forces, with the protection of their planes, maneuvered comfortably. They were about to encircle us.

Then, to my shock, I saw the commander of my Battalion and his helper, Captain Verrini.

There was nothing left to do but retreat. The major said, "There still remains a couple of hundred meters to be enclosed."

We began to cross the rocks. We managed to take ourselves out of the circle and reorganize the troops. Evening came and the German units returned to their bases. We took advantage of that to attack, forcing the enemy to retreat toward the town of ARGOSTOLI.

After about an hour of combat through the narrow streets of Argostoli, the Germans were forced to give up. We captured about 500 Germans, including their commanding officer.

Half an hour later, two German landing craft from LIXURI attempted to dock in port. But, before reaching their goal, they were annihilated by our batteries. The landing craft was shattered. The port was a bed of corpses.

On the night of the 15th, the 500 prisoners were taken to the concentration camp in VALSAMATA.

The next morning, my division returned to the camp. In the afternoon, the 6th company departed to attack a group detached in a village called EKALA. From dawn until dusk, German planes continued hammering.

That same day, the Battalion of the 312th infantry had attacked German troops in the area of AYRAPATA. We suffered casualties.

On the morning of the 16th, the platoon in which I was a part left to guard the prisoners. On the morning of the 18th came the order to leave by truck to reach AYRAPATA.

Along the way, we were attacked several times by aircraft.

We came to EMOEMYA. We dispatched troops in several areas. We hoped to engage in combat with the defender. But, this did not happen.

In the evening, I was ordered to go on patrol and scope out a town about two kilometers away. We heard the blasts of ammunition. With information obtained by explorers, I entered the town. The incendiary firings of the Germans allowed a clear view of the area.

I came to a house and knocked on the door. A woman appeared at the window. She looked frightened. She said that the Germans had run away half an hour before we arrived. Before leaving, they plundered and raped.

Many of our soldiers and civilians lay dead on the ground.

I returned to the command and relayed everything I had learned. The next morning, I left on a second exploration into the same area.

Despite knowing that we were Italians, the population was afraid to leave their homes. Some of them welcomed us. While crying, they recounted what had happened in their homes the night before.

They showed us where the bodies lay of our soldiers who were killed in combat. After being taken prisoner, many of our soldiers had been shot by the Germans.

In the afternoon on the same day, the order came to move. We went to a location where two other Italian Field Battalions had arrived. There, they dispersed and broke ranks in a deep valley a few hundred kilometers from the front. Our Battalion had a rifle company, a gunners' platoon and a mortars platoon. It was commanded by Captain Ciaiolo.

At the time of the attack, we had the task to climb over the 3rd Battalion and assault. For three days, we were under continuous machine gunning. Fortunately, the valley was a large shelter from aircraft.

Navy Lieutenant Commissioner SOLITO and Captain CIAIOLO fell in combat in Cephalonia.

On the evening of the 20th, General Gaudin, Commander of the Brigade, and General Gherzi, Commander of the Division, arrived on site. The two looked at the area, studied war plans and departed. That night came the order to attack at 7:30 the following morning. I was called by my captain. He gave me the order to form a patrol and stay in contact with the 2nd Battalion.

At 6:00 in the morning, my company commander spoke with Colonel Dara. I showed up with my patrol to ask for my orders. But, before I could say anything, I heard German gunfire. The captain pulled out his gun, threw himself to the ground, and began to fire. "Fire, boys! Fire, Rasile! Take that gun and courage! The Germans have taken us by surprise!"

Lying on the ground with the musket under my belly, I took aim and fired.

Hand grenades choked me.

I kept shooting.

The fight did not give me much hope.

Then I saw a possibility that I thought would save my neck. It was a difficult maneuver, but I had to try.

The Germans were many and were approaching us from above. We were placed in an unprotected trench. I tried everything possible to move to my left where the road passed over a bridge. On all fours, after much effort, I was able to maneuver under the bridge and rejoin the fight.

I went out to the edge of the bridge and continued to shoot at the target. The fight was escalating. Through the thick smoke, I saw my captain. He, with a bloody arm, was being held up by two soldiers. Only then, the captain gave orders of surrender.

I hid under the bridge. There, I found an officer from my company and my comrade staff sergeant. The lieutenant wanted to move out from under the bridge and surrender. We objected by saying that if the German column would pass without us being seen then we were free.

The last soldier of the column had the task to rake the area. Two drivers left the column and went down in the valley where there had been fighting. From there they could see us hidden below the bridge. One of them signaled us to come out from the hole with his rifle. *What could we do? Resist and get killed?*

Given that choice, no one could still be useful to their country.

The following story was not in the journal. It was handed down orally.

On the island of Cephalonia, after his company had been destroyed, Alessandro and a few other soldiers managed to escape.

While on the run, for one night, they hid in a merchant's store. The owner provided Alessandro and the others with food and shelter.

The merchant's child was present. Alessandro remembered thinking how innocent the child looked, and how, in war, all innocence seemed to be lost.

FOUR

Prisoner of War

September 1943, Italian soldiers of the Acqui Division were taken prisoner by the Germans in Corfu. We gave ourselves up. A German with the face of a convict searched each of us. I passed the Inquisition. He took away my gold chain that I had around my neck, a pocket watch, and a fountain pen. I almost preferred to have him kill me than for him to take all of my possessions.

Since I was unable to thank him with two punches in the nose, I cursed him.

The Germans took us with them. After 100 meters, we found another ten Italians. They made a signal for us to form into file with those in front of us. There were armed guards ready to give the coup de grâce if anyone got out of line. We thought that there was no hope of saving ourselves.

I commended my soul to the Lord and prayed together with my fellow sufferers. Some tears appeared in my eyes, blurring my vision. My thoughts were of my dear mother. *Who knew how she would suffer not knowing what had happened to me?*

I despaired, thinking that this was the end.

After a while, a German approached me. He made a sign for me and my comrade Benedict to come out from the ranks. We gave him our backpacks. He put them on his shoulders and had us follow him. They had radio transmission equipment strapped to a mule. While we walked, I saw that some others had been pulled out of the ranks and recruited to carry ammunition boxes. Looking at my comrade, I said, "Hopefully, God has just saved us all from a fate of the damned."

The terrain was mountainous and rocky. We had to walk where and how they told us or else they would not hesitate to blow our brains out. We would often hear gun shots without knowing what was going on.

After about half an hour's walk we stopped, unloaded the equipment from the mule, and began communications.

When the Germans finished their communication, the equipment was dismantled. The large transformer (used to charge the batteries) was loaded onto my shoulders. It took two people to load it onto me. My bones creaked from the great weight.

We started again, marching up and down the mountains. The heat made us drenched with sweat. We got drunk from hunger and thirst. I was foaming at the mouth like a horse.

Evening came and we found ourselves in a village called VALSAMATA. Our torturers found a cottage where a poor family lived. They forced the family to leave so they could sleep in the beds.

My friend and I had to sleep outside. We feared wolves. Despite our weariness, the fear kept us on our feet all night.

Later, one of the Germans called to a Greek woman and ordered her to give us something to eat. The poor thing, having nothing else, gave us a slice of bread and some dried olives.

We spent the night with the Germans because we feared what would happen if we tried to escape.

In the morning at dawn we started again with the same weight on our shoulders. They took us to a village called MARUPATA. There, they resumed communications with their planes that bombarded the island.

At two o'clock in the afternoon on September 22nd the fighting stopped. The Germans had no more need of our help. Having no more orders, they told us to continue to the city of ARGOSTOLI.

After walking about one kilometer, we found many of our Italian soldiers already disarmed. I approached an officer and asked if there was anything to eat. He indicated that a small distance away there was a warehouse. He said, "There you will even find a small bit of rice that we prepared before being taken prisoners."

So, we went to stave off the hunger by finding the rice. Other soldiers took booty from the warehouse.

After eating, we rummaged in the warehouse for some provisions. We arrived just in time to find some jars and a canteen of oil. Within walking distance of the warehouse and along a wall lay on the ground four German artillery officers who were shot in the back by their prisoners. The corpses were face down. They did not have on a jacket or boots.

My inner voice told me that the prisoners would shoot everyone. So, I agreed to escape into the mountains to rearm with them. While considering our next move, a German troop ordered us to accompany them to the town's concentration camp.

Many of us slept outdoors. Sleeping on the ground was not pleasant. Thankfully, the season was warm so being outdoors wasn't that bad.

The first couple of days we were fed well. This soon ended. The Germans gave us a biscuit and a ladle of hot water. Then, even this meager ration was removed. We were starving. Day after day, our force was wasting away. Our morale was very low.

The German guards didn't allow any civilians to approach who might want to help us with a small piece of bread. Sometimes they threw us quinces to eat. We had to boil it with seawater. We saved the drinking water because they gave us only half a liter a day.

Since the Germans were not allowed to shoot us they wanted to make us die from hunger.

After a few days in a concentration camp, a soldier came from my company. His name was Pietro Luccadamo di Cosenza. A few days earlier, he had been captured and taken prisoner.

He told me that when the German troops discovered his fellow soldiers and him they took all of them from the gatehouse, including the officer. The Germans lined them up at a pit and shot them. He and another soldier called Maurizio Usai di Sardinia, in early rounds of gunshot, threw themselves into the pit. They were covered by dead bodies. When it was over, they climbed out, soaked with the blood of their brethren.

They found some clothes and changed. The officers then headed along the cliffs by the sea to the other side of ARGOSTOLI. A few days later, they presented themselves to the concentration camp.

Thousands of our soldiers were lost during the battle of Cephalonia. About twenty officers, including a Captain of the Carabinieri, were in camp with us, held for questioning. One morning at dawn, these soldiers were taken by truck to Santo Teodoro where, along with several others, they were shot.

Our morale lowered because every day more of our comrades would arrive with more stories describing the fate of our poor brethren.

One of those stories was from a chaplain, Padre Romualdo Formato, one of the seven chaplains of the Acqui Division.

THE CHAPLAIN'S TALE:

The officers go out and line up in front of the wall of a small solitary house. A platoon of German soldiers puts their helmets on and aims their submachine guns.

The officer's fate is now clear.

The chaplain who accompanied the officer Striesto tried to persuade the German NCO leading the team to not kill the Soldiers.

The chaplain was rejected.

The Chaplain tapped the Red Cross insignia tied to his arm and again begged for their lives.

"Bah," one of the non-commissioned officers sarcastically responded. "You speak of the Red Cross in the fifth year of the war."

One petty officer yelled, "Send out another eight!"

Out filed another group of officers.

The Petty Officer angrily gestured, implying that he wanted a smaller group. "What kind of discipline do you have in your army?"

The German soldiers took aim at the officer's heads and fired. Each officer fell from the blow.

"Send out another eight."

Knowing that they are going to die, the officers bravely faced their death. Only a young second lieutenant burst into tears and yelled, "Mother! Mother! How are you going to survive alone? "

The chaplain quickly gave his attention to each one as long as he could. He received short wills and objects to be delivered to distant relatives. He gave an extra word of encouragement to the condemned.

The German thugs then tore the victims from the priest's arms.

The German Officer said, "Don't have time to waste. The schedule includes a swim in the sea at noon and immediately after a good meal on the beach."

And what would happen to us? Perhaps a fate worse than a gunshot. But, there remained hope that the war would soon end. Germany alone could not continue much longer.

FIVE

Sympathy from Greeks

One day, I saw in front of me a face that was familiar. It was a friend of mine, Alessio Rasile. It had already been two months since he had arrived on the island of CEPHALONIA.

We passed those hard days in each other's company, talking about our homes and our families to distract us from the hunger. From time to time, he would pray. With much patience, we found the best ways to endure our hardships.

On the 2nd of October, the Germans loaded some of the prisoners onto a trailer and sent us to the mainland to the city of PATRAS. But, as they sailed out of the port (or so they said), they hit a mine and were blown to smithereens. Almost all our soldiers died because the Germans did not let them out of the hold.

On the 3rd day of October, the Germans asked the men for volunteers to make a second expedition. But, seeing the misfortune that happened to the men the day before, everybody pulled back.

I called to my friend and asked him, "I am going. Are you with me?"

Concerned, he looked at me and said, "Aren't you afraid you'll become feed for the fish?"

I responded, "We don't have any other choice. Let's take a risk with the hope of going somewhere where we will find someone who will have mercy on us, or else

24

we will be sure to starve. Let's go and we will see if God assists us."

Quickly, I took a backpack full of rags that I had, and reached the group of volunteers headed to the port to embark. Of course, it was hoped that before leaving we would get something to eat.

Those hopes were in vain.

In single file, they made us climb aboard a three-mast motor sailor. On board, there was a German officer who shouted at the damned. "Run, Run!" Occasionally, he would hit us with a whip. I couldn't see why we had to receive those lashes.

Shoving us toward the hold, we had to be careful when we jumped to seize the rope. Otherwise we would fall to the floor below. Sliding down the coarse rope, we flayed our hands.

After he had dropped a good number of us, the fierce German Officer came down. Red faced and with eyes closed, he lashed out without worrying where his whip might land. He pushed us all on one side of the hold to clear room on the other side for our companions to come down.

When the hold was full like sardines in a can, the officer (dog that he was) went up and started the same system, assigning men to the other two holds.

Once full, the boat left port.

When will we arrive? We were wondering. *Where are we going?* Nobody knew anything.

After a few hours standing, we began to tire. We felt the need to sit down to rest. But, it was impossible to sit because we were too tightly squeezed together.

As night fell, hunger and thirst tormented us. But, the Germans wouldn't give us a drink of water. Locked up in the hold, the heat choked us. Some fainted. Others wanted to go to the bathroom. Unable to move, they re-lieved themselves where they stood.

The Germans wouldn't even know if anyone died. Indeed, they were amused by our suffering.

The journey was long. We spent two days and two nights in that jail. None of us had any more strength to move.

On the morning of the 5th of October, we finally felt the drop of the anchor.

We felt some relief as we realized that it was time to get out of that hell hole.

Eventually, the Germans gave orders for us to come out. They dropped a ladder. They assisted us at the top of the ladder to step onto the deck.

We were at the port of PATRAS.

We descended from the deck. In file, we were taken to a barracks that was about three kilometers away.

Crossing the town, the Greek civilians looked at us with concern. Our faces showed the signs of dehydration and hunger. Not long before, we had been the enemies of Greece. Now, they felt sympathy for us.

Along the way, women, men, girls and Greek children approached us to give us something. Girls, with aprons full of sliced bread and money, opened their linens to offer us something. The German guards would not permit them to cross the line, occasionally indulging in volleys of automatic weapon fire.

Armed with machine guns, the Germans were stationed every fifty meters. They would shoot at civilians who tried to reach us prisoners.

We arrived at our destination, which was enclosed with double rows of barbed wire. On that day, we went without food. Hunger had weakened us to the point that none of us could remain standing. We had to descend the stairs leaning against the wall.

I would often remember what my father would say about his dealings with the Germans during the First World War. There was no more barbarous people than the Germans.

The next day, we were given a kilogram of bread to be divided among twenty-four people. The day after, they gave us twelve kilograms. Then, they would give us a soup per day. It was mostly water with a few leaves of vegetables.

Day by day, we wasted away.

SIX

Losing My Pictures

On the 15th of October, we set off from PATRAS by train. The morning of the 16th we arrived in ATHENS. We walked for many kilometers to reach the camp. It was located just beyond the Acropolis.

The Greeks tried to give us bread, but the Germans did not allow any civilians to approach.

In the concentration camp of ATHENS there were prisoners from several nations: Italians, Russians, British and Americans.

In this camp, our treatment improved...somewhat. They gave us a little more to eat. This happened because at that time the I.R.C (International Red Cross) was visiting the camp. Having the I.R.C there was a great relief. They gave us hope.

Since I was a sergeant major, I was given the command of about 200 Italian prisoners.

On the 25th of October, we departed ATHENS on foot headed to PIRAEUS.

In the evening, we embarked on a steamer. The German crew of that ship was even more wretched and irresponsible than the crew of the last ship.

We boarded in single file. An arrogant German threw us down into the hold like dogs. Some bent over in time to cling to the rope. Like pieces of salami, others fell to the floor.

When my turn came, I made sure I had the rope in sight before he gave me the boost. I clung to the rope and

28

went down slipping. My hands were flayed. With bleeding hands, I landed on a few of my colleagues. In the darkness, I lost my beret and backpack, which contained some of my rags, documents and photographs.

The next morning, I searched the hold, hoping to find some of my documents. None turned up. I could not find even a photo. For two days, I searched in every corner. I could not find any trace.

On top of this, I began to be tormented from hunger. The ration was a biscuit and a can of 100 grams to divide among four people. This had to sustain us for twenty-four hours.

On the third night at sea, I felt as if I was dying of thirst. Since the time we boarded, the Germans had not yet given us a drop of water. The heat was suffocating. I had shortness of breath.

My friend, Alessio, was worried about me. He asked for a few drops of water. There was none to be found. We were all under the same conditions.

The Germans did not permit us to leave the hold. We didn't know why.

Finally, I couldn't take anymore. Little by little, I felt my respiration diminish. Then, I had the idea to urinate and drink it. And that is what I did. I closed my eyes and drank. I eventually began to feel better.

The next morning, thinking we were going to die from hunger and thirst, we argued with the German dog for food and water. Those rogues further disrespected us by throwing the buckets of drinking water on us, soaking us from head to toe. Then, they filled the buckets with sea water for us to drink.

I thought we would never see the end of this persecution. Hunger, thirst and covered with lice that tortured us more than the Germans, we had to have the patience of Jesus, especially since we thought we migh end up as martyrs like him.

SEVEN

Unafraid of Death

After four days and four nights at sea, on the 29th of October we arrived in THESSALONIKI.

After everyone was out of the hold, I looked once again for my documents. But, I could not find them, not even a trace of a photograph.

I climbed the ladder and disembarked with my companions. As we crossed the streets of THESSALONIKI, we saw shops that sold every grace of God. Some had white bread. In other shops, there were smoking hot dishes on tables piled high with macaroni. We became drunk from hunger.

About a quarter of an hour later we arrived in a concentration camp along with other rebel slaves. They gave us some soup, a little piece of bread with some butter, and a bit of jam. The next day, the food was the same.

On the third day, the German camp commander rallied us all and asked if we wanted to keep working with them in the Balkans. He tried to persuade us with false promises.

At one point, I could not take any more of his nonsense. I said, "Commander, on behalf of everyone, I say, and let me put this in your head once and for all, we, your prisoners, are rebels and we prefer death than to cooperate with you."

The officer took out his gun and fired at the ground near my feet. I wasn't afraid of him killing me. Death would be a relief from my suffering.

Finally, he said, "I would kill you like a dog, but I think it would be too easy to let you die by gunshot. Instead, now you will be treated like beasts struck with a stick. You and your families won't ever see each other again. Soon, you will be taken to RUSSIA where there is extreme cold. There, you will shovel snow."

His words didn't intimidate us. We were accustomed to the hunger and would also get accustomed to the cold.

On the 11th day of November, we were given showers and received disinfection. In the evening of the same day, we were placed in freight cars, forty-two people in each. Stored like cargo, a thousand Italians prisoners were bound for White RUSSIA.

EIGHT

White Russia

I was appointed wagon Chief, responsible for the distribution of the bit of bread they gave us. The doors of the wagons were opened once a day to either pick up food or, for someone who felt they would die, to hopefully draw a bit of water if they had the good fortune to find some where the train had stopped.

At the stops, the guards watched us closely.

Oftentimes, in the station there were twenty-five wagon loads of beets. Though hungry, we couldn't do any touching for the cost was too high. The Germans could kick us with a blind rifle shot. But the hunger was un-bearable so we ate boiled potato skins. After suffering stomach pains, we ate dirty stems of cabbage. We ate it, not caring if it was garbage or not.

We couldn't endure hunger for long. Through the bars of the windows, with the train crew, we would look for opportunities to exchange some of our rags for a piece of bread. But we already had almost nothing to exchange. Many were left without their underwear. At night, their teeth would chatter from cold. The lice ate us alive with-out compassion.

One day, we arrived at a station in Poland. The train stopped to pick up food. The Polish population be-gan to approach the train. When they saw that we were Italian prisoners they crowded around the wagons with baskets of bread.

Girls from ages sixteen to twenty, with baskets full of bread, were crying and asking the guards to let them approach the wagons to give us food. The Germans had hearts hard as stone and would not let them get close.

Eventually, the locals made the decision to shove themselves forward and approach us, pushing pieces of bread through the windows barred with barbed wire.

We admired the good heart of the Polish population. Even though it was only bread they gave us, it helped fill our stomachs.

The next day, the windows were nailed over with shingles. So, we now had no light and little air.

After two hours, the train continued moving.

We spent twenty-one days locked in that freight car.

Finally, we arrived at our destination: BORISSOW (White RUSSIA).

Italia - Alesandria 1·3/20-5-40

Evacuation of German troops from the Port of Pillau, April 1945

NINE

Becoming a Shoemaker

On the 2nd of December, in the morning, we departed the train. They took us to a large concentration camp about three kilometers from the station.

The cold was unbearable, especially to those of us who were unhealthy and poorly dressed. The day we arrived in the camp we were showered, received disinfection, were distributed a soup of barley without seasoning, and were assigned to a barracks that fortunately was heated by a large stove fed from a keg of gasoline.

The next day, they took us to an office where they recorded our personal information, including our profession. They also took a copy of the fingerprint of our right index finger.

We received a wooden badge that indicated the number of the camp, our prisoner number, and our profession. Then, they sent us back to our cabins.

I wrote down the profession of shoemaker. I thought this would allow me to be inside away from the cold. It was a good idea because on the 12th of December they called the category of shoemakers and tailors. Each group consisted of 100 people. They took us about two kilometers away from camp to a location that was led by a German company of the 4th army.

The Germans oversaw the clothes warehouses for the army with a tailor who worked with 100 people. This 100 workers included civilians, women, men, Russian prisoners, a cobbler with about 60 civilians, and others who worked in the warehouses.

On the first day of travelling with this company, we ate well. But the following days the dream changed and the reality was the usual ration of boiled wheat.

For five or six days, we worked in the clothes warehouses. The cold dropped below 37 degrees. Although we had the opportunity to wear clothing like furs, sweaters and gloves, there was no remedy from the cold. Only a warm place would have benefitted us. Otherwise, jackets were good for nothing.

We slept in a barracks adjacent to that of Russian prisoners. It was fenced off by barbed wire. A second row was located around all the warehouses and laboratories. In the evening, the sentries would lock the door to our cabin and reopen it in the morning. They would then accompany us to work. After five or six days, we were taken to work in shoe-making. There, we had a chance to steal from the Germans. As a result, we were also able to get some small pittance from the Russian civilians.

We started to run contraband. Our bellies began to feel better. We knew we were taking a risk because, if the Germans found out, they might hang us unmercifully. Hunger did not know risk.

The Germans were not so dumb. There were more soles disappearing than those used to repair shoes. For a month, when the chief cobbler closed his accounting he was always short one hundred to three hundred pair of boots. He did not believe that we could steal all that material. He was able to convince those when questioned that he was in good control of the incoming material.

Since the German sentries could not take whatever they wanted from the warehouse, we did some contraband with them. They turned to us prisoners for new boots, sweaters, hats and whatever else we were making. We made out well, having a few pieces of bread to fill our stomachs. The Germans realized our trafficking began to go through the shop when we left from the warehouse, but we made suckers of them anyway.

Every now and then one of us would end up in a dark cell. Fortunately, the commanding officer was understanding. He realized that we could not live with the small rations they gave us. He would soon release us from that dark cell.

The Germans did not notice that our work was worthless. No shoe was assembled properly. With many small pieces of wood, we would assemble a pair of soles. Most found that they could not stand in those shoes for more than half an hour without them falling apart. Often, we would apply a knife to the leather so water could get in.

In the shop, only the Chief Cobbler could cut and rivet uppers. This cobbler, a German Marshall, was very useful to our cause because he was against the government. So, everything proceeded in our manipulation of the German forces.

During the Christmas party in 1943, we were given a quart of cognac to divide among four people. We were also given sixty cigarettes and two packets of candy. At Easter, they did not give us anything and we had to work all day.

We spent six months in BORISSOW. We did well with trafficking contraband. We were in relatively good health. Because of our risktaking, we could have easily ended up on the wall being riddled by German bullets. But, the good Lord lit our way and guided us always.

TEN

The First Retreat

Russian troops were rapidly advancing.

On the 28th of June came the order for retreat. Our Sergeant interpreter rallied us together and took us to the clothes warehouses.

He said to us, "Take what you need because to-morrow the warehouses will be burned."

On the 29th, we gathered to march. We were Italian and Russian prisoners. We were given some food and we left on foot, headed toward MINSCH.

We were accompanied by our interpreter and some guards. A few kilometers from MINSCH, we changed course. The town was on fire and surrounded by Russian troops.

The streets were crowded by retreating German troops, civilian prisoners, and an endless supply of trucks and tanks.

We spent the night in the outskirts of MINSCH. Russian ammunition and rockets bombarded the city without relief. Occasionally, we heard the cries of women. The poor Russian families who were evacuating were not left in peace by those barbarian Germans.

At dawn, we resumed the journey without knowing where we were going to lay our heads. My feet had become bloated and full of blisters. We had used all our provisions. Hunger made itself felt. We had to make do along the road, giving clothing to civilians in exchange for a few pieces of bread.

Although the season was favorable for sleeping outdoors, the nights were cold.

Each day, we advanced 100 kilometers on foot. In the morning of the fourth day, it appeared that we were surrounded by Russian troops. We found ourselves outside the gates of the town of MOLODEZSCHI. The guards who accompanied us twice made us retreat a few kilometers back because the circle was closed. Around noon, German troops succeeded in opening a space of two kilometers. Then, we had the order to cross the city. When we came to the first houses, the German guards deserted us.

A few minutes before we arrived, the town was bombed. Now, the town was in flames. The streets were a bed of smashed corpses, horses and mules. Many of them were roasting in the flames. The smell of burning meat was nauseating.

We knew the Russians were worse savages than the Germans so we did not want to be captured by them. For that reason, we decided to cross the town and get out of the circle. The maneuver wasn't easy since none of us knew the terrain.

The shots and cannon fire of Russians was heart wrenching.

We each made the sign of the cross and began to run through the streets of the city. Everywhere it was raining cannon fire. The warehouses, all in flames, emitted a hellish heat. The sweat from our forehead down to our feet flowed in buckets. Blistered feet wrapped in rags didn't allow us to go fast. Dust and smoke choked us.

The train station in the center of the city was filled with wagon loads of ammunition and incendiary weapons, which when set on fire erupted, sending bullets of every caliber in every direction. This explosion sent large wooden beams and pieces of shrapnel in every direction.

It took a long time to walk through the town. At one point, I felt as if I could not breathe as my heart began to beat more rapidly.

A German Marshall motioned me to mount a horse, which he had tied around a post. I did not hesitate. I mounted the horse, gave it a kick with my heels, and began to gallop across the city. Occasionally, we were met by German tanks which maneuvered through the town square. The noise disturbed the horse. It raised on two legs. After going a good distance, I was forced to descend the horse and resume running.

After about two hours of running, I made it out of the town. There, I found friends, or rather fellow sufferers. I threw myself to the ground, exhausted. I rested under a grove while our other companions arrived. But, not all arrived. Some were destined to rest eternally among the ruins of MOLODEZSCHI.

After stopping for a quarter of an hour, we decided to continue. Orienting ourselves with a small magnetic compass that I carried with me, we took route.

After a stretch, we found a river to cross. But, the bridge had been blown up. Without loss of courage, we undressed and tossed the shoes to the other side of the river. We threw ourselves into the water and swam to the other side.

But, once on the other side, before we could get dressed, we were attacked by the Russian rebels. Mistaking us for Germans, they unleashed hellfire, whistling down bullets over us like lightning. Thankfully we were protected by a high road.

Swinging around, I was stunned to find near my feet a bicycle. But, it had no tires. In the blink of an eye, I mounted that bicycle and raced like a madman along a path beside the road. After going a couple of kilometers, the hellfire ceased.

I caught up with my companions who had outran me. Hearing more whistling bullets, we stopped to decide on the best course to take. Looking into each other's faces we asked, "What should we do? Remain hidden in some ditch?"

But, we understood that those advancing would clean out all Germans. There would be no saving ourselves. It was impossible to remain in this hell. We'd all be mistaken for Germans.

We commended our souls to God. We prayed that he would illuminate our way and save us from harm. Suddenly, a short distance away, a train loaded with German war material was ready to leave the station. We rushed to join it and climbed into the wagons, hiding under the material on board.

After a few minutes, the train departed, headed for the town of WILNA. That night stealth planes gave the alarm. The train stopped. We climbed down and fled into the countryside. The planes began to drop incendiary clips. Soon, the train's load of material was on fire.

In the morning, we met with personnel from the train and put ourselves on the path to WILNA. After four days and nights of walking, on the evening of July 6th, we arrived in WILNA.

At night, we stopped on a hill next to a cemetery. A short distance from us, about 150 meters away, was the railway station. But, even here, before midnight, hell was unleashed. Bombs dropped continuously and machinegun fire bit the station. An endless supply of rockets lit up the town as if it had been midday.

The bombs filled the air with that humming sound made by bees.

As dark as that night was, there was a lot of light, which made the sky look like day.

In the morning, the city was still in flames. We could see people in the streets. They were terrorized with fear. Dust-covered people emerged from under the rubble with pale, haggard faces. They were dazed, a look of disbelief in their eyes.

In the morning, we went to the train station. Thankfully, it had not been too badly damaged. We were able to take the train to the town of GRODNO. On the 8th day of July we entered that town. After a two-day stopover, we departed by military transport. After more than twenty kilometers of road, we arrived in a town called AUGUSTOV. There, we were assigned to a subsistence troop whose job was to unload and load material. We had access to every kind of food: bread, jam, butter, and many other types.

We looked for a chance to steal. We often suffered lashings, but lashings did not fill an empty stomach so we were willing to take the punishment in exchange for food.

On the 18th of July, we set off from AUGUSTOV. On the 19th we stopped at CHELIMBURG. That same day, at four in the afternoon, ten people including myself left to go to the city of LICK, which bordered Poland.

Arriving in LICK we had to unload ten wagon loads. We remained there to work in the clothes warehouses. We were well treated in Lick. We were given the same food and the same rations as that of the German soldiers.

On the 5th of August, we left LICK and traveled to a little town called PACCINDORF. The following day, six of us were assigned to work for a large agricultural land baron whose business was the harvesting of wheat. This new master, a wretch, made us sweat from 7 in the morning until 8:30 at night with very little to eat. We complained to our captors, but our protests fell on deaf ears.

On the 18th of August, our captors sent us to again work in shoe repairs. Returning to the village, we found that the cobbler was about one kilometer from our camp.

The first time the guards accompanied us because they did not trust me with the responsibility of taking my comrades to shoe repairs alone.

In the village, there was no lack of beer. Often, as we crossed the town, the guards would make the rounds to drink a few glasses of beer. Although prisoners, the civilians knew we were Italians by our actions. Everywhere we went we were admired and respected.

Russian troops were advancing.

After a short time, the civilians began to evacuate. On the 3rd of December, we set off from PACCINDORF and went to another village called CLACHNDORF. In this town, the Germans had established a big clothes warehouse and a factory for shoe repairs. The cold was getting harder to bear. But, working in shoemaking, we didn't suffer much.

As Christmas approached, we thought that amongst us prisoners we would organize a small theater in our barracks to distract us from bad thoughts. Getting permission from our German captors, we found everything we needed, including costumes taken from the stores in the village. On Christmas night, we filled our barracks with many viewers: women, men, civilians and prisoners.

Applauded by all, the spectacle went well. When the spectacle was finished, we danced all night to music performed with accordion, guitar and mandolin.

The next morning, the German commander, who had not been invited, learned of the party. He ordered that the windows be barred, double guards posted, and that the barracks be locked up in the evening at eight and only opened in the morning for us to go to work.

For eight days, the guards accompanied us to work.

On the New Year holiday, we again made the theater inviting the same guests. This time the German Commander didn't say anything.

It was January of 1945. The Russian front was approaching.

ELEVEN

The Second Retreat

One morning, the Germans gave the order to pack everything. The warehouse full of clothes was emptied and distributed to the civilian population. We loaded wagons with sweaters and other items of clothes. We walked along the streets to distribute the clothes to civilians and prisoners.

It looked like a market.

We thought that the war had ended. But, of course, it had not.

On the 26th of January, accompanied by guards, we set off from CLACHNDORF.

None of us knew where we were going.

The roads were covered with snow. The cold was unbearable. Walking on the snow every day and night nonstop through blizzards was exhausting.

Occasionally, the exposed skin of our faces would freeze. We would immediately rub our skin with snow. Through the suffering, we forced ourselves forward, making superhuman efforts so as not to be abandoned and left frozen in the snow.

After about sixty kilometers we arrived at night in a village called MELSBACH.

The guards who accompanied us had orders to hand us over to the concentration camp. After three hours of standing on the street in the cold, they managed to find a barn where we could rest.

The next morning, instead of taking us to the camp, we were assigned to work at a crop farming company. The first two days we had to empty two stalls full of straw so they could be filled with food. They gave us very little to eat. Our strength lessened more and more.

On the third day, the 2nd of February, a friend and I were too weak from hunger to get up and go to work. It had been days since we had eaten. We hid in the attic under the straw. From time to time, we would poke our heads out to see if we could get food from a civilian. But, there was a military column of vehicles in the road preventing civilians from passing by.

It was about ten o'clock when we started to hear the noise of tanks, the sound of clips, and incendiaries falling. With an infernal racket, these bombs shattered the roof of the barracks. In the twinkling of an eye, we were covered by broken tiles and wooden beams.

Without hesitating, we ran out and threw ourselves onto the horses. Blood dripped from the horse's wounds. My friend had a wound to his head that dripped with blood.

"Are you hurt?" I asked.

He didn't think so.

We took off before another round could give us a death blow.

We reached the road that headed out from the town. Using a package of medication I had in my pocket, I treated my friend's wound with bandages.

We were dumbfounded by how we had been able to get out safely from under that hell. We were convinced that it could only have been a miracle of God who had saved us.

The next day we went to work in the warehouses. There, we had the chance to supply ourselves with food.

Eventually, we left the camp.

On the night of the 5th, we arrived in BRAUSBERG. It was about two at night when we crossed the town (we traveled at night to avoid the danger of bombings). After a few kilometers, we arrived at a large barracks and hospital. We complained about the cold, but our complaints fell on deaf ears. We had to wait on the road until dawn.

At the crack of dawn, four engine bombers appeared. We took shelter in the basement of the hospital. It was full of sick people. The first bombs fell on the hospital. Many fell in the courtyard, which was crowded with carriages and horses. The basement was shaking like there was an earthquake. A friend of mine was wounded with shrapnel in his arm.

After about half an hour the planes departed.

We emerged from the basement. There was one remaining carriage with a horse. We took it and fled through town.

Throughout the day, even in the countryside, we were subjected to aerial machine gunning. Fortunately, there were no casualties.

In the evening, we were led to a village about two kilometers from BRAUSBERG. We stayed there for many days, working according to where we were needed.

Days later it was learned that the company (A.B.A 515) to which we belonged was in ELLIMBERG, about 20 kilometers away. Our interpreter convinced us that it was in our best interest that we rejoin the company.

So, after a few days, we started to work in shoe-making. In addition to shoe-making, we were forced to load the warehouses. Like beasts, we worked night and day.

Each night a group of forty people had to unload sixty to seventy trucks of clothes full of dirt and blood. The smell was unbearable. If any of us tried to get out of work we were beaten.

It was hell. We could not continue in that way. Fortunately, food was everywhere in that area. In every house there was potatoes and ham left behind by the civilian population that had been evacuated. This was a great relief because, with the addition of those heavy jobs, the hunger would have killed us.

In the middle of March, the bombing began.
The Russian front was close.
We foresaw that we would become encircled by the enemy. Targeting us night and day, they wouldn't leave us in peace. We didn't have any shelter because they didn't give us time to ourselves to prepare. We didn't know where to hide. Russian artillery shots came from all sides.
Russian troops had arrived on the outskirts of the city. There was no way that we could escape without encountering danger.
We needed to reach the port to embark on ship so that we could reach the other strip of land and the town of PILLAU.
The port where we needed to embark was controlled by Russian artillery and planes, making boarding very difficult. But, we had to take the risk. To stay where we were was certain death.

TWELVE

Reunited with a Friend

On the night of the 20th, despite the rain of continual gunfire, the Germans made us dig trenches. We did this on the 21st and 22nd as well.

Over our heads circled hundreds of planes that unceasingly bombed us. As soon as we dug out the trenches, the Germans would get in and be sheltered. We stayed exposed.

We could not see through the smoke and fire. Everywhere clods of Earth would fly up. The area within a radius of a few kilometers around us seemed like a volcano erupting. The ground swayed like the sea.

It was hell.

After half an hour of bombing, the town of ELLIMBERG was leveled.

In the evening, we finally received the order to retreat and for us prisoners to be sent by ship to PILLAU. This news raised our hopes. With the terror we experienced that day behind us, we hoped that we would leave before any further danger appeared.

In April of 1945, the German troops evacuated from the Port of Pillau.

Russian artillery fire had not yet ceased.

At one point, they made us stop working and sent us to the shack where we slept to get our stuff.

Our cabin was unrecognizable. Tanks had punctured the walls. In front of the door lay the cadaver of a German soldier. It was headless.

Inside the cabin everything had become a mound of rubble. We walked in and dug among the wreckage to find some rags.

We left in a hurry under continual fire. We joined the Italians under the German command. We were given something to eat. Then we marched towards ROSESBERG about two kilometers from the port.

Around 500 meters before the port, we stopped to wait for a transport to be readied for us to embark. But it was difficult to embark under the constant shelling. All night the missiles lit up the harbor, making the night as bright as day.

Later that night, the conditions became good enough to cross the channel. There was heavy fog so there was no danger that our transport would be sighted.

Meanwhile, the pounding of artillery continued from all sides. The port was crowded with soldiers, civilians and prisoners.

Every grenade safely missed its target. But, to embark without anything happening seemed impossible.

It was midnight when we got the order to go to the port to embark. We each made the sign of the cross and quickly moved across the village.

The streets were crowded with vehicles. In every street, there was a bed of corpses. Our hearts beat more strongly from witnessing the horror.

Clutching my Rosary as I was hustling to reach the port, I prayed God would save us from any danger. I begged him and all the Saints.

The thought of such a horrible death scared me. My thoughts flew to my parents, especially to my dear mother. Her name was every moment on my lips as I muttered, ' Mom! Mom! Who knows if I'm going to see you again!"

Thankfully, the good Lord illuminated our way. All Italians reached the port safely. By the seat of our pants, we jumped on the transport. I praised God with all my heart that he had saved us from further harm.

After two hours of sailing, we arrived at the port of the town of PILLAU. There, we were taken to the concentration camp where we found other Italian and Russian prisoners.

In this camp, food rations were bad. Each day we were sent into the woods to dig trenches and unload ammunition. We walked twelve kilometers a day.

In this last camp, I met with one of my dearest friends, Sergeant Enrico Ricciardi. He was part of my own regiment. This meeting was a joy for us since we had always been together.

We followed the same course for a few months. But, one day in June 1945, fate would separate us forever.

My dear friend fell ill with a case of typhus. Within a few days, he died. He was buried in the cemetery of GUMBINNEN.

In the camp of PILLAU, all was not peaceful. At night, bombers would come close to the camp. One evening, two Italians were wounded by shrapnel from a bomb which fell meters from the camp.

Our cabins were made of wood. Bullets fired from machine gunning planes easily put holes in the walls and ceilings as if they had been made of ricotta cheese.

Our hearts continuously pounded in our chests.

We couldn't escape.

Our camp was secured by a barbed wire fence. The enclosure was patrolled by watchmen who were guarding us.

There was no way out.

We had to stay in our cabin where we thought we would be killed by Russian shells.

THIRTEEN

Building a Shelter

After eight days, we were transferred to work in a forest a few kilometers from KONIGSBERG.

There, the jobs were tough. At night, we were taken to the seashore six kilometers away to download troop carriers loaded with building material. During the day, we removed stumps to build trenches for Germans. We also made huts for their accommodation.

The gun fire poured down like rain, especially on the nights when we went to unload boats. The Germans stayed in a village in the countryside. Before it was too late, we thought we should build a shelter to be safe from shrapnel.

We were able to dig a spot under a big shrub. We were a group of about ten people. It took us a few days to build the shelter. We dug during the few minutes a day they gave us for rest. After a few days, the refuge was very useful.

One night, about a dozen silent planes began to circle above us, sending incendiary phosphorus bombs everywhere.

Seeing what was happening, we prepared for the worst, working well into the night to reinforce our refuge.

On the morning of April 15th, a Russian reconnaissance plane passed overhead, leaving a streak of smoke in the form of a circle.

It was easy to guess what it was doing.

It was identifying a target to bomb.

After a few minutes, there came a squadron of four-engine planes. They began the bombardment. But, in addition to the squadron of bombers, there were hundreds of light planes that flew over at low altitude strafing and firing at the ground.

In our shelter, there were fifteen people closed in like anchovies. The clatter of the bombs caused in us so much nervousness that we were not able to stand still. We did not feel safe anywhere. We were trembling like leaves. The planes were causing a furious clatter as hundreds of bombs fell. We couldn't run away from the planes flying at low altitude.

The ground was flipped by bombs. All the buildings were destroyed. Only one small house, thirty meters from our shelter, remained intact.

To come out safe from that hell was a miracle.

Our cabin was already in flames.

Shortly after, that last little house was shattered.

Huddled against each other in that shelter reciting the Holy Rosary, we didn't have much hope of getting out safe from that danger unless the good Lord protected us.

An entire day went by without being able to put our heads out from the refuge.

It was almost sun set.

The bomber formations were not yet satisfied. They wanted to make one final shot.

We felt a large flutter of bombs falling. Holding our breath, we made the sign of the cross and resigned ourselves to death. But God would not permit it.

Many bombs fell around us. We were almost suffocated by the dust and smoke of the bombs.

When the planes finally departed, we emerged from the pit. With great amazement, we noticed that our shelter had been crowned with a great hole caused by the incessant bombs. The village had all but disappeared. The bombs left nothing, only flames and cleared land.

God had put his hand on us, protecting us once again.

We all gathered to leave that place. A few Italians were missing. Others were injured.

At sunset, the storm had ceased.

FOURTEEN

Sleeping with Horses

Accompanied by guards, we started on our journey. We walked all night to the town of PILLAU. Nocturnal squadrons did not want to leave us alone along the road. They accompanied us with clips and phosphorus incendiaries.

After a couple of hours of walking, we arrived in a village called FISCIAUS. Having been bombed that same day, it was all in flames.

Again, came the blows of the Russian artillery.

We walked for fifteen kilometers. We arrived at a hospital along the coast where we had orders to stop. It was two o'clock in the morning. Hungry and tired, we were loaded into a hospital corridor and told to sleep.

At dawn, a dull hum of a squadron penetrated our ears. I called to my friend Ricciardi and told him, "So begins another day. What do we do?"

We didn't have much time to think about that. We abandoned everyone and ran on our own. Otherwise, we would have become a pile of bones.

Eventually, my friend asked, "What course should we take? Do we head to the town of PILLAU and find something to eat?"

I answered, "God will provide."

"But we don't even have a morsel of bread!" Ricciardi exclaimed.

I said, "Dear friend, we should not lose courage. Along the road we are sure to find dead horses so we're not going to die of starvation."

The first squadrons appeared as we left along the sea coast.

We distanced ourselves a few kilometers as the first bombs fell in the area that we had just left. We heard the blasts of ammunition. We saw earth raised by bombs and thick columns of dense smoke.

"You see that?" I said to my friend. "The Lord guided us along the right path."

Under a railroad bridge, we found a bucket filled with ricotta. The ricotta was enough to take away our hunger for that day. The squadrons were bombing without mercy the entire strip of land that bordered the sea. They gradually came closer to the town of PILLAU.

The sky was clouded by an infinite number of planes. We ran like mad to reach a place where we could find shelter. From time to time, we were attacked by machine gunning. But, along the coast, there was an embankment with a deep ditch providing good shelter.

In the evening, we reached the town of PILLAU. There was a concentration camp for Polish civilians, Russians and Germans who were waiting for deportment. There, we presented ourselves to the German police, hoping to receive something to eat. But, they would not listen to us.

So, we went to beg from the women who were in the camp. But, they too were hungry.

We were able to get a few slices of bread. After we ate, we went to sleep in a stable with horses.

The next morning, we awoke to canon fire. We always carried with us some tools to build a little shelter. We thought to move a few kilometers from where we were and build a shelter.

We found a good location.

While three of our comrades were building a shelter, my friend and I thought of going around in search of food. We approached a hospital hoping to collect the leftovers of the sick.

There, I saw a horse who had under his snout a bag of peas. I took off running with the bag of peas back to my comrades. We threw a party. Shortly thereafter, five fellow sufferers arrived. Our group was now twelve.

After working for a few hours on our shelter, we realized that nearby there was a bunker. We threw open the door and descended into a vast shelter where there were many chambers providing protection from bombs. But, unfortunately, they were filled with German soldiers who wouldn't let us stay.

While crossing the town, a brigade of Russian tanks launched a barrage of cannon fire.

Under the crumbling station, we found shelter. But, after the barrage, we continued. We eventually found a broad and strong shelter. But, it was already occupied by Polish girls and young civilians. Some were wounded. We asked them if we could join. They were happy to have our company.

Although the room was large, we were not comfortable since we were about twenty people. But, we adjusted the best we could to cause as little inconvenience as possible.

At the Station, trains on the tracks were full of all kinds of food. We were able to feed our thin skins.

We remained there eight days.

One evening we were found by German police. We said that, following the heavy bombardment on the 15th, we had been separated from the group. We were ordered to surrender and head immediately to the port to embark on ship to STUTTHOF.

We had hoped to stay there and wait for liberation by the Russians. Instead, we were threatened with death by the police.

Under guard, we left and headed to the place to embark.

The night was silent.

Planes were flying overhead.

After an hour's walk, we arrived at the port. But, there were thousands of people waiting for the ferry to take them across to the other side. We managed to cut in ahead of the crowd.

After fifteen minutes, we landed at NUOWAUSE, another strip of land near GDANSK.

There, they told us that a few kilometers away there was a concentration camp. We walked all night. The next day, we walked all day. After sixty kilometers, we found the famous camp of STUTTHOF.

In the camp, we found between a hundred and a thousand French and Italians.

Everyone had a hole in the ground to sleep, even us.

FIFTEEN

Leaflets from Above

Over the next few days, more prisoners arrived. In this camp, we could die from hunger. We had to split a kilo of bread among twenty-eight people. Every now and then they gave us a chance to leave the camp in search of dead horses to carry back to the camp. We would eat these horses, even without salt. In time, we even found ditches with potatoes. This enabled us to survive the days.

Things were going worse and worse for the Germans. The Russians were advancing quickly and the front came closer and closer. Assuming the worst, they gave us the authorization to report to the camp because it was safe from bombing by aircraft.

Seeing that they were beginning to be a little more interested in our welfare, we thought the Germans were winding down. But, around the camp the Germans ignored reports that told them they were safe. Only meters away from the camp, they had us form a barrier of artillery pieces. Russian bombers at low altitude tried their best to raid our camp. But, it wasn't easy. They tried to bombard the German artillery. Many times, bombs came to visit us in the camp.

On the 8th of May, the sky was clouded with aircraft. They were flying at very low altitude to spy on our camp. Some bombs were dropped in our camp, causing eleven deaths.

Afterwards, they dropped leaflets into our camp. The leaflets said that if by midnight the Germans had not surrendered they had orders to destroy the entire camp by shelling bombs. It did not matter if there were prisoners still inside.

With the concern that we would be destroyed, we began to work like cattle to build shelter for protection. But, it was all in vain.

The German artillery fire was bedazzling, flames shooting continually from the mouth of every weapon. Despite this effort, it was said that at midnight the Germans would quit fighting. In fact, at a few minutes to midnight the firing stopped.

The next morning, it was announced that the war was over. It seemed too good to believe. It seemed impossible that these stubborn Germans (led by another stubborn young General of twenty-four years) would have finally realized that it was useless to resist after the massacre at ELLIMBERG and PILLAU. In the meantime, we continued to work to strengthen our trenches.

But, shortly thereafter, everyone was leaping with joy. It was true.

The war was over.

SIXTEEN
The Death of Innocence

Without wasting time, we jumped over the fence and went out to look for food in mountain huts that had been abandoned by the Germans. We found a good supply of canned food, butter, bread, tobacco, other types of food and amenities.

At 9 o'clock, the first Russian Cavalry patrols arrived in the area where we were. A Russian officer came into the camp and told us that soon we would be deported. We prepared to leave the camp the following day.

In the morning, we set off on foot, accompanied by the Russians, heading toward the town of ELBING.

After seventy kilometers of walking, we arrived in ELBING. The town was in ruins. But, there were a few factories still standing at the outskirts of the town. We stayed a few days in ELBING.

We were a group of a thousand Italians. There was five thousand Soldiers between French, Belgian and Slavs.

On the 13th of May, we were to leave ELBING. We walked 210 kilometers. But, before we departed, my friend Palma and I thought to go ask the Russian leadership if they would give us authorization to take command of the thousand Italians. In this way, we would not need to take orders from a French captain. The Russians agreed to our request.

In a few minutes, we gathered all the Italians. We ordered them to find carriages and horses in the camp

70

that the refugees left behind. Being smarter than the French, we took ninety carriages and 120 horses, while the French only took thirty carriages. This was enough for supplies and their wounded.

So, with food for us, we went on horseback and carriage. None of the Italians needed to walk on foot.

The first day's march was met by an accident. A spooked horse charged out of the row. The rider thought to save himself and jumped. He hit a tree limb, striking his head. After a few minutes, he died.

On the 17th of May, we stopped in the outskirts of LANDSBERG.

In this town, there was an endless number of corpses. We were suffocated by the bad smell.

Within walking distance, there was a church. We visited. In a small room adjoining the church, there were two dead. Their heads were separated from their bodies. They were killed by those who perhaps hoped to find some treasure.

Climbing the stairs of the bell tower we noticed a foul smell. We suspected that there were corpses. But, the more you climbed, the landings became tighter. They failed to show any dead.

I wanted to climb to the top landing of the bell tower. But, as I climbed the last steps, I became frightened by what I saw. A girl, who I think was eighteen or twenty years old, was stretched out on the landing, fully nude. Her flesh was still vital. A lock of blonde hair covered her shoulders.

Her body, battered and swollen, had bruises all over it that were caused by bites and punches. She had a stab wound. It was horrible to think about how that girl suffered. The wretch who committed that violence should have been burned instantly by God.

I knelt, made the sign of the cross, and called upon the Lord that he would never again allow a man to commit a crime like that.

After the prayer, I went down the stairs, dumb-founded by all that I had seen at such a young age. I was only twenty years old.

SEVENTEEN

The Russians are Worse

On the 22nd of May, we arrived in the town of GUMBINNEN. There, we found another 2,000 Italians, including some officers.

I lead the column on a white horse. On a stick, I had attached a huge Italian flag that I had hidden since we had been taken prisoner.

Upon our arrival, all the Italians who had been brought to that town greeted us with a big rally. We stayed for six months in GUMBINEN.

We tried to arrange meeting places, theatres, dances and sports to distract us. But, the Russians were more terrible than the Germans. They regarded us as slaves. They sent us to work in minefields. They gave us almost nothing to eat. The little food they gave us was so bad that we could not eat it. So, we would find ways to steal wheat and potatoes from nearby farms.

My dear friend Ricciardi was admitted to the hospital with typhoid. After eight days, he died.

In that period, there were many cases of typhus. The Russians didn't try to save anyone. They didn't even bother to provide the sick with a typhoid injection. I began to hate those Russian wretches worse than I hated the Germans.

I was ordered to assume command of a company of Italians, 180 men. Every morning, I had to accompany them to work. They worked in the fields to harvest grain and potatoes.

The work was very dangerous because the fields were mined. The Russians were not concerned for our safety. They treated us worse than the Germans.

For several months, we struggled with this harsh life. The French, fifteen days before the end of the war, were repatriated. But we Italians never saw the end.

We were subjected to many interrogations by Russian GPU. Every day they took away some of our companions without us ever knowing what became of them.

Of those of us that came from GUMBINEN, many developed a strong case of typhus. Our friends were dying every day.

Finally, on the 30th day of September came our order for repatriation.

We went to the station to take the train. But, we were disappointed to find that the train was only for transporting Russian material. So, we set off on the 1st of October at 2 pm.

On the same day, we stopped for a few hours in ISTAMBURG. The next day we continued. On the 7th of October, we came to Frankfurt. On the 8th of October, we set off from Frankfurt. On the 9th, we arrived in Berlin.

On the 10th of October, we set off from Berlin and passed through GERA, a town important for its factories and establishments of all kinds. On the night of October 14th, we crossed the Brenner Pass. The morning of the 15th of October, we stopped a few hours in BOLOGNA. We then continued to TRENTO. At VERONA, we had a rest stop. The next day we set off from VERONA by way of the BOLOGNA- RIMINI RICCIONE line. We stopped for two days due to a broken bridge. On the 20th day of October, I finally arrived home.

ALESSANDRO RASILE

This story was not in the journal. It was passed on orally.

After GERA, we went to ZURIK (AUSTRIA). The Russian authorities that accompanied us handed us over to the American military authorities, which after welcoming us with care and respect, gave us food, cleaned us and disinfected our personal items.

The next day they put us on the train to cross the Bremer Pass to VERONA where we were presented to the Italian authorities. They sent us home where I arrived on the 20th of October 1945.

EIGHTEEN

Finally Home, Struggles Continue

A few days after my return, I had to present myself to my military district to be declassified. At Rome's territorial defense, I was assigned the classification of prisoner, first category.

I submitted the form for unlimited license awaiting employment for reenlistment. I spent four years waiting to be pressed into service. Often, the district asked me to provide additional information. In four years, I was contacted six times. My request was never answered. In this period, Twice, I presented myself to the Latina Military District to be pressed into service.

I explained to the District Commander Colonel that having lost my parents because of war and having no more home because the Germans had blown it up, I needed him to show some understanding for a wretch like me. It was all in vain to the Colonel who, without showing any emotion, said to me, "Get a job."

I thanked him and told him that, where many who have thought only of themselves have lived with indifference in the face of those who sacrificed for the nation, I served the King with many years of sacrifice for my country.

In 1949, I asked the Latin Military District for expatriation. I was told that they couldn't release that document to me because my military position had not yet been adjourned.

ALESSANDRO RASILE

These uncaring people who occupied important offices were without conscience.

CONCLUSION
The Girl from Greece

Manhattan, 1968

While recovering in the hospital, a nurse intern walked into Alessandro's room. When she saw him, she looked surprised. She smiled and said, "I recognize you."

Alessandro had no idea who she was.

The nurse went on to explain that she grew up in Cephalonia. Her father was a merchant who owned a small store. She said she remembered Alessandro and a few other soldiers hiding in her father's shop. He gave her father a gun to protect himself and his family from the Germans who were quickly overtaking the island.

Shocked, Alessandro looked at the nurse in disbelief. He was surprised that she recognized him after such a long time.

Looking into her eyes, Alessandro could see that little girl who, over twenty years earlier, had been in that store on the island of Cephalonia. In those eyes, he was glad that he could still see some innocence.

After the girl from Greece left his hospital room, Alessandro never saw her again.

Rosa Rasile's 90th Birthday

Most of the Rasile family

Alessandro and grandson, Adam

Captain John Mingo

38425401R00046